THE FANTASTIC WORLD OF
Baby Animals

LEARN

FUN FACTS

SIZE

WEIGHT

LOCATION

AGES 3-10

Jackie Noble of
San Diego Humane Society

FUN FACTS
About Our
Cute Friends

About the Author

For more than a decade, I have devoted my time to helping the most vulnerable baby animals at **San Diego Humane Society**. At the organization's nursery, we have provided care to thousands of kittens, puppies, and even piglets, bunnies, and ducklings! As the Director of Nursery and Placement, I have the honor of coming to work every day to help baby animals grow, heal, and - when they are big enough - find adoptive homes.

As far back as I remember I was passionate about animals, especially baby animals. When I was 4 years old I got my first family pet, a tiny tabby kitten named Mittens! Mittens the kitten had wispy whiskers, stripy sides, a tiny tail, and four little white paws which was the inspiration for her name. After Mittens became part of my family, I loved animals even more and wanted to learn everything about them. I went on to study **Zoology at the University of Glasgow, Scotland**, and graduated with a master's degree.

In addition to my job, where I get to be around baby animals all the time, **my passion for animals has taken me around the world**. I have traveled

to see giant pandas in China, lions and penguins in South Africa, sea turtles in Belize, and hippos and elephants in Kenya.

I can only imagine how much I would have adored the fun facts and incredible images in this book as a kid! From fluffy fur to fuzzy feathers, baby animals are truly the cutest, and in this book you will get to learn about 18 amazing species.

Science has proven that looking at pictures of cute baby animals can trigger positive emotions and improve your focus, so read this book often and please enjoy! Whether you are a child or a grown-up reading along, I hope this book **inspires compassion** toward animals and sparks your love for the most adorable animals of all, the babies.

Jackie Noble
Director of Nursery and Placement
San Diego Humane Society

To learn more about San Diego Humane Society or to donate, visit sdhumane.org

African Lion / Cub

Panthera leo

Gestation: 3-4 months

FUN FACTS

Lion cubs are born and raised away from the pride for the first month. In this time, they play with siblings, learn to walk, and gain strength before they return to the pride with their mother.

Cubs are born with their eyes and ears closed.

Lion cubs have spotted fur to help them stay camouflaged. This keeps them safe from predators, and as they grow up, they lose their spots.

All female lions in a pride help raise the young, and cubs can nurse from any adult lioness.

Cubs start to hunt for themselves at 2 years old.

Where do they live?
Savannas and grasslands in Central, Eastern, and Southern Africa

How big are they?
3-4 lbs
12 inches long = 2 game controllers

What do they eat?
Mother's milk, eat meat at 3 months, weaned at 6 months

African Elephant / Calf

Loxodonta africana

Gestation: 22-23 months

FUN FACTS

Elephant calves are 3 feet tall and weigh about 200 pounds when they are born. They will drink 3 gallons of milk a day, and the weaning period can last for up to 10 years.

Calves are born with poor vision, so they recognize their mother by sound, touch, and scent.

Female elephants have the longest pregnancy of any mammal at 23 months.

Calves must be able to stand just a few minutes after they are born in order to feed on their mother's milk.

Calves can be very clumsy since much of their behavior is learned, including how to control their trunks.

Where do they live?
Savannas and forests of sub-Saharan Africa

How big are they?
260 lbs
3 feet tall = a scooter

What do they eat?
Mother's milk, start eating plants at 4 months. The weaning period can last for 10 years

Hippo / Calf

Hippopotamus amphibius

Gestation: 7-8 months

FUN FACTS

Hippo mothers will give birth to their calves in an isolated area away from other hippos. She leaves for up to two weeks, and this will give her a chance to bond with her calf.

Even when they are on land you can see their ears fold and nostrils close when they suckle.

Baby hippos can nurse underwater.

Baby Hippos can be born in water, but they can only hold their breath for 20-40 Seconds. So, the mother must push them to the surface.

Mothers will remain in the water with their baby calves for several days before the calf's legs are strong enough to walk on land.

Where do they live?
Primarily found close to rivers and lakes in sub-Saharan Africa

How big are they?
60-110 lbs
4.2 feet long = a bicycle

What do they eat?
Mother's milk, chew on grasses around 1 month, graze at 5 months old, and fully weaned at 1 year old

Mountain Gorilla / Infant

Gorilla beringei beringei

Gestation: 8-9 months

FUN FACTS

Baby gorillas are called infants, just like human babies. However, they are much smaller than human infants when born, weighing only about 4.5 lbs while humans weigh about 7.5 lbs.

For the first several months, a gorilla infant will be held and carried by its mother. Once they are strong enough, they will hold on to their mother's back, shoulders, or belly.

Young gorillas can be very active, play-fighting with each other, and sometimes an adult silverback gorilla (400 lbs) will gently join in.

We share 98% of our DNA with gorillas which makes them one of our closest living relatives.

Young gorillas will continue to share their mother's nest for up to 6 years.

Where do they live?
The mountains of Central Africa

How big are they?
4 lbs
10 inches tall = a tablet computer

What do they eat?
Mother's milk, start eating some vegetation at 2.5 months, but will continue to nurse until they are 3-5 years old

Harp Seal / Pup

Pagophilus groenlandicus

Gestation: 3-4 months

FUN FACTS

Harp seal pups gain roughly 5 pounds per day thanks to the high-fat content of their mother's milk. This helps them build blubber for warmth and fat reserves when the mother goes hunting for food for up to six weeks at a time, where the pups can lose half their body weight.

Pups will start to molt their baby fur after 4 weeks. They will molt several times while growing up until they develop darker fur like their parents.

Pups are born white to camouflage against the pack ice while their mothers are out hunting. Their white color also absorbs heat from sunlight.

Pups won't enter the water to hunt for themselves until they are about 2 months old.

Harp seals most commonly give birth to one, and twins are incredibly rare.

Where do they live?
North Atlantic and Arctic Oceans

How big are they?
**25 lbs
30-36 inches long = a skateboard**

What do they eat?
Mother's milk until they reach 80 lbs, and then they eat small fish and crustaceans

Sea Turtle / Hatchling

Chelonioidea

Gestation: 9-11 weeks

FUN FACTS

Sea turtle hatchlings have one of the most challenging upbringings of any animal. Their chance of survival to adulthood is about 1 in 1,000. Hatchlings will emerge from their nests in the sand at the same time, and they will race to the ocean as they face danger from predators, pounding waves, and disorientation from non-natural light sources.

They are born on a beach buried in nests with up to 1,000 sibling eggs and grow up without their mother.

The temperature of the nest determines whether they are males or females. Warmer nests produce females, cooler nests produce males, and middle-range nests create a mix.

Adult females that are ready to lay eggs will always find their way back to the same shore they hatched from, even if they have not been there for 30 years.

The hatchlings that make it into the ocean will drift and wander alone for about a decade until they are big and strong enough to forage along coastal waters.

Where do they live?
Circumglobal in warm and temperate waters

How big are they?
1 oz
2 inches long = a battery

What do they eat?
Mollusks, crustaceans, seaweed, jellyfish, and fish eggs

Emperor Penguin / Chick

Aptenodytes forsteri

Gestation: 9-11 weeks

FUN FACTS

Emperor penguin chicks are born into one of the harshest environments on the planet. Early care for chicks is successful by a collaborative parenting effort between the mother and father who take turns feeding and warming the chicks.

It takes 50 days until chicks can regulate their own body temperature.

When chicks are born they only have a very thin layer of down which is not enough to protect them from the extreme cold environment, so they stay close to their parents for warmth.

The fathers will have fasted for 4 months while they incubate the eggs and wait for the mother's to return with food.

The mothers spend two months hunting in order to build up food reserves that they use to feed their newly hatched chicks.

Where do they live?
Antarctica

How big are they?
11 oz
6 inches tall = a hot dog

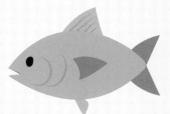

What do they eat?
Regurgitated Fish

Giant Panda / Cub

Ailuropoda melanoleuca

Gestation: 3-5 months

FUN FACTS

Panda cubs are born hairless and pink in color. They require a lot of attention from their mother, and this may result in the mom not eating or drinking for several days at a time.

At 1-2 weeks old the classic black and white fur starts to make an appearance.

Cubs won't open their eyes for the first time until about 55 days after birth.

At about 2.5 months old a panda cub will begin to crawl, and it takes nearly 6 months for them to walk.

Panda cubs are the smallest known newborn mammal when compared to their mother's size.

Where do they live?
Temperate forests of the mountains of southwest China

How big are they?
3-5 oz
5-7 inches long = a banana

What do they eat?
Mother's milk and then bamboo at 6 months

Black Bear / Cub

Ursus americanus

Gestation: 4 months

FUN FACTS

A mother black bear can have anywhere from 1 to 5 cubs at a time, though 3 is the most common. Cubs are taught by their mother at an early age to climb trees to escape potential predators.

When cubs are born they weigh half a pound, do not have any hair, and won't have their eyes open.

Cubs will not emerge from their mother's den until the spring when they will weigh about 5 pounds.

They will remain with their mother for about a year and a half before they set out on their own.

Cubs are born in their mother's den during the winter, and they will nurse on her milk until spring.

Where do they live?
North America from Alaska to Canada to Northern Mexico

How big are they?
8 oz
8 inches long = a soccer ball

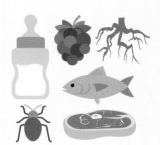

What do they eat?
Mother's milk, nurse until fully weaned at 6-8 months old. As they grow up they will eat a mix of berries, roots, fish, insects, and meat

Wolf / Pup

Canis lupus

Gestation: 9 weeks

FUN FACTS

Wolf litters will include 4 to 6 pups called littermates. This family will form a pack with their parents and older siblings from previous litters.

Pups are born with their eyes closed, and will open them for the first time after 10 to 14 days.

Pups will begin hunting with the pack at about 6 months of age.

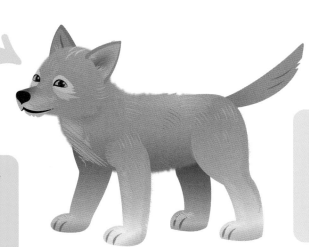

Wolf pups are born in a cave or den, and remain there with the mother for about 1 month before coming out for the first time.

Playtime is also learning time for wolf pups. They will actively play with all members of the pack, and this helps build hunting skills that they will rely on throughout their lives.

Where do they live?
North America, Asia, Europe, and North Africa

How big are they?
1 lbs
6 inches long = a dollar bill

What do they eat?
Mother's milk, fully weaned by 8 weeks. They will grow up to hunt rodents, hares, deer, elk, and moose.

Dog / Puppy

Canis lupus familiaris

Gestation: 8-10 weeks

FUN FACTS

Dogs are descendants of wolves and have been a long-standing best friend to humans, but did you know that relationship first formed about 29,000 years ago? The pets we have in our homes today are referred to as "domesticated breeds."

Puppies are born with their eyes and ears closed.

Puppies will sleep 15-20 hours a day.

A puppies coat or pattern darkens as they get older. A dalmatian puppy is born white, and the black spots start to come in at 10 days old. Other breeds with spots/speckles do this too.

The first dogs were domesticated from wolves, but today there are 360 recognized breeds of dogs.

Where do they live?

All around the world, except the arctic

How big are they?

2.5 oz – 1 lbs
3-8 inches long = a pencil

What do they eat?

Mother's milk, start weaning around 3-4 weeks. Then they move on to approved and appropriate dog food, and meat treats

Cat / Kitten

Felis catus

Gestation: 8-10 weeks

FUN FACTS

Cats have also been a long-standing companion to humans, but their domestication time is less certain, ranging from 10,000 - 14,000 years ago. Since this relationship formed, cats have been held in very high regard among human civilizations, and even considered sacred in ancient Egyptian culture.

Kittens are born with their eyes and ears closed.

Kittens eat every 2-4 hours.

All kittens are born with blue eyes, and they start to change to their adult color at 4-5 weeks old. By 10-12 weeks their eyes fully change to their adult color.

Today there are 71 recognized cat breeds in the world.

Where do they live?

All around the world, except the arctic

How big are they?

3-4 oz
3 inches long = a crayon

What do they eat?

Mother's milk, start weaning around 4-5 weeks. Then they move on to approved and appropriate cat food, and meat treats

Horse / Foal

Equus caballus

Gestation: 11-12 months

FUN FACTS

A baby horse is called a foal. A male foal is called a "colt," while female foals are called a "filly."

Foals are mostly born at night to protect them from predators, and the birth can take place in a matter of minutes.

Horses and humans have a very long relationship throughout history that dates back roughly 6,000 years.

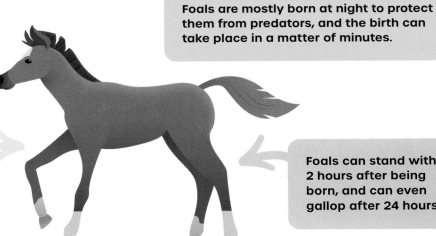

When born, a foal's legs are almost as long as they will be when they're an adult.

Foals can stand within 2 hours after being born, and can even gallop after 24 hours.

Where do they live?
All around the world, except the arctic

How big are they?
100 lbs
28 inches tall = a tennis racket

What do they eat?
Mother's milk, start to eat grass at 2-3 weeks, fully wean at 4-6 months

Cow / Calf

Bos taurus

Gestation: 9 months

FUN FACTS

Cows are very intelligent and have good memories! They can recognize and remember other cows and even the people they meet. Cows are social animals and enjoy living alongside other cows for companionship, calves especially like being in physical contact with other cows.

All calves are born with horn buds, which will harden and grow into full horns, but it is common to have them removed after birth.

Baby male cows are called "bull calves," and baby female cows are called "heifers".

Cows are born with baby teeth, and it takes between 1.5 to 2 years for them to grow their adult teeth.

A calf can stand and walk an hour after birth.

Where do they live?
All around the world, except the arctic

How big are they?
60-100 lbs
28-30 inches tall = a baseball bat

What do they eat?
Mother's milk, wean at 6-10 months old. They will start eating grass as early as 2 weeks old

Pig / Piglet

Sus scrofa domesticus

Gestation: 4 months

FUN FACTS

Pigs and piglets are very intelligent animals. A piglet can learn its own name and even learn tricks quicker than a dog.

Piglets are very hungry, and they can double their weight in a week.

Mother pigs, called sows, are very loving and nurturing and will "sing" to their piglets when they are nursing.

Pigs and humans have a much longer relationship than horses. Evidence shows pig domestication occurred 9,000 years ago.

Pigs have an extraordinary sense of smell, proving to be about 2,000 times better than humans.

Where do they live?
All around the world, except the arctic

How big are they?
3.4 - 4.5 lbs for domestic pigs
6-10 inches tall = a party hat

What do they eat?
Mother's milk, eats plants at 4 months, weaned at 3-6 years old but can suckle for up to 10 years

Rabbit / Kit

Oryctolagus cuniculus

Gestation: 4-5 weeks

FUN FACTS

Rabbits have been pets to humans for thousands of years, but there is still debate as to whether rabbits are in fact domesticated.

A baby rabbit is referred to as a kit, which is short for a kitten.

Baby kits are born pink and hairless. They start to get fur at 7- 12 days old.

Kits feed on milk only 1-2 times a day as their mother's milk is rich enough to sustain them for up to 24 hrs.

Rabbits can have 3-4 litters per year, with up to 15 kits in each litter.

Where do they live?
All around the world, except the arctic

How big are they?
1 oz
2 inches long = a battery

What do they eat?
Mother's milk, wean at 4-6 weeks old, and then feed on a variety of grass and plants

White-tailed Deer / Fawn

Odocoileus virginianus

Gestation: 7-10 months

FUN FACTS

Fawns are born during the early summer which allows them to blend into, and hide in, surrounding vegetation.

The white spots make the fawn extremely hard to spot for predators. Their spots fade as they grow, and by 3-4 months old they are mostly brown.

A fawn can stand up within 10 minutes of being born.

Mothers will leave their fawn alone for long periods of time, only checking in to nurse them. This is done because the fawn is much safer alone since they do not have a scent, and they are more camouflaged than their mothers.

After about 3 weeks the fawn will begin to travel and feed with their mother.

Where do they live?
North America in Canada, the United States, and Central America

How big are they?
4-8 lbs
15 inches tall = a bowling pin

What do they eat?
Mother's milk, start eating some vegetation at 2 weeks old, and fully weaned at 12-16 weeks old

Duck / Duckling

Anas platyrhynchos domesticus

Gestation: 4 weeks

FUN FACTS

Ducklings hatch from an egg, and there can be up to 15 eggs in a clutch. Although eggs in the same clutch can be laid days apart, all the eggs will typically hatch within a 12-hour period of each other.

Ducklings have a pointy bump on the tip of their beak to help them crack open their shell when it's time to hatch. This is called an "egg tooth" and falls off a few days after they hatch.

Ducklings are born with a fuzzy and fluffy down coat. They will have this for about 6 weeks until they grow their first feathers.

Ducklings will not feed for the first 24 hours, but after that, they are capable of feeding on their own instead of being fed by their mother.

Once the ducklings hit 8 weeks their wing feathers will be developed enough for them to make short flights.

Where do they live?
All around the world, except the arctic

How big are they?
1-1.5 oz
2.3 inches tall = a birthday candle

What do they eat?
Plants, fruit, grasses, crustaceans, worms, snails, and insects

CLAIM YOUR FREE GIFT!

Visit

PDICBooks.com/Gift

Thank you for purchasing
The Fantastic World of Baby Animals,
and welcome to the
Puppy Dogs & Ice Cream family.

We're certain you're going to love
the little gift we've prepared for you
at the website above.